Sacred Goddess Poetry

The Collective
A Soulful Mind

by

Helen Rigby

Copyright © 2021 Sacred Goddess Poetry, The Collective *A Soulful Mind* by Helen Rigby

All rights reserved.

No part of this work may be reproduced, stored in a retrieval system, or transmitted in any form or by any means, electronic, mechanical, photocopying, recording, or otherwise, without the express written permission of the author except in the case of brief quotations embodied in critical articles and reviews.

ISBN: 978-1-7369709-0-4 (paperback)
ISBN: 978-1-7369709-1-1 (ebook)

Cover Designer: Jana Mariz Templo, M.D.
Logo Designer: Jana Mariz Templo, M.D.

Coming Soon!

Other books by Helen

Nadine's Sunflower
Fall 2021

The Goddess Guide to Chronic Illness
Spring 2022

Visit www.helenrigby.org to be notified when new books by Helen are released.

Author's Note

This particular body of work began nearly a decade ago. After writing poetry on and off for close to twenty years, I finally decided I would commit to writing poetry every day and see if anything worthwhile came out of it. Nearly one year to the day since I made that commitment to myself, I get to share my first poetry book with you. The Collective *A Soulful Mind* pays homage to these last few decades that I've spent hiding away from the world.

In this first full Sacred Goddess Poetry collection, I've written about the daily struggles of living with multiple chronic illnesses including: endometriosis, trichotillomania, interstitial cystitis, as well as, the mania, depression, and anxiety of bipolar one. The struggles with my chronic illnesses and my mental health are the main driving forces behind the collection. However, I wouldn't have fully committed to this journey if it wasn't for the traumatic physical injury I sustained in March 2020. Many of my poems discuss the impact that this too has had on my body and mind.

Of course, like many poetry collections, you will see work discussing what we gain and lose in the world of love and loss. Stubborn hearts and those that we can't let go of.

My only hope with putting my work out on display is that you, the reader, get something meaningful out of it. That perhaps you are left pondering your own existence, the relationship you have with yourself, and how you show up in this world. I hope this book reminds you of your strength, resilience, and creativity. You are truly capable of incredible things. Never forget that.

– With deep gratitude,

Helen

Contents

Part I
The Catalyst

Part II
The Invisible Wars

Part III
The Rise & Fall of Love

Part IV
The Place Where Great Spirits Meet

Part V
The Sacred Goddess

Part I

The Catalyst

Post Surgery

An ocean of tears
soak my pillow as
Pain swallows
my body whole

I go to scream
but I'm choked
With silence
I try to breathe
But my lungs are
shards of glass
Refusing to function

The metal hardware
that plagues my body
Has turned me into a
creature unrecognizable

The cold steel
pierced my chest

Creating a void within
my body that begs
To be filled
with more than
Crippling loss

Burning its way down
from my eyes
The salt water
fills the rest of my body

Betrayed by my own tears
I'm not weightless
This is not a calm water
carrying me to safety

This water drags me
to the depths of
My pain overtaking
me completely

This turbulent ocean
this endless agony

Is a symphony of knives
slashing through my vessel of flesh

Sleepless nights and
dark creatures wait for me
Calling me over
with a wave of their hand

I dare not ignore them
or they will hunt me down
They will feast on my body
without warning

3am decisions

The pain

Will kill you
or
Transform you

Let this
be your call
To action

You decide

Become the butterfly
or
Decay in your cocoon

A Feast Fit for Kings

The titanium rod
The metal screws
The broken spirit
The agony

Feed the treacherous gargoyles
I've had to carry
a true feast fit for kings

They merrily sit around their table
it's quite the spectacle
a joyful sight to behold

This gathering of beasts
keep me up
long past the hour
my old body could handle

My body
morphs into
a block of stone
they begin carving
their meal
out of me

Too many questions
enter my mind
when I'm back
in my cage

Do I have a hand
involved in this?
this feast of flesh
and soul

Am I betraying
my own body?
by keeping the lights
on for them

How do I get myself out
of this forsaken dungeon?
how do I break free of my chains?

No knock to warn of
their entrance they
barge their way in
then take me back
to the king's table

I wonder what part of me
they'll devour tonight

Desolation

It took everything
each part of me
I spent years polishing
and accepting slid
Out from underneath me
in the matter of three
Seconds there is nothing
of the old me left

I look in the mirror
and I don't know
that face that body

I was stripped down
to the bones

That so easily
crumbled under
The weight of
sorrow and suffering

My spirit shattered into
a thousand pieces
Any future dreams
now gone

Any promise of
a brighter day
Now broken

Foundations

The foundation of my world
has fallen away
Crumbling under the
weight of time and space

The foundation of my body
is rendered useless
Cruelly my bones have
fled for not even they
Could hold up
my now empty soul

I Tried to Walk Today

I tried to walk today
how silly am I
my body must have thought

For my legs are now
papier mâché and
sadly only fraught

With pain and weakness
there's nothing left to say

I'll try again tomorrow
to try to walk today

Percocet

What you came to tell me
I do not know

For you do not know
how to soothe my woes

So quickly did my
Dream decide to end
joyfully the nightmares
Began again

You looked at me
tears in your eyes
The love we had
now in disguise

You tried to speak
but no words came out
Where once was love
there now is doubt

I tried to hold
you in my arms
But the nightmare started
and you turned to yarn

11:15pm

    100 milligrams of Seroquel taken at 10:08 pm. The restlessness begins to stir my body. It awakens my dreamless mind. It has to be at least 2am perhaps 3am? I check my phone and it reads 11:15pm. I am awake. Heart racing. My mind alert. Is this anxiety? Who let you in at this hour? I was on my way out. Hoping for genuine rest. Where did you even come from? You're far too generous with your presence. I honestly don't know if I should cry, scream, or laugh at the obvious lack of connection between my brain and body. How long will this last? Trapped in a body that refuses to rest. Paired with a tortured mind. This sleepless wasteland has become too familiar. The welcome back sign is blinding at this point. I can't help but find this amusing and tragic at the same time. It must be the pain meds and approaching midnight hour who find this entertaining. With no trace of the Seroquel left in my body I heave myself up. "This doesn't make sense", echoes in my mind as I wheel myself to another room. Those words are too familiar for many reasons right now. The thought of increasing my dose enters through the now open door and then swiftly makes its exit. "No. This has weighed on you mind, body, and soul for years

now". Words that I don't want to repeat aloud yet force myself to. My body in excruciating pain. My stomach being assaulted by invisible knives. It feels as if there is no end to this torment. The slight haze is lifting, so I decide to write. Perhaps this startled slumber came from my guides nudging me to create, to pour this out on paper. Perhaps this is just addiction and rejection at its finest. Whichever this is, I must accept. Looking out through the midnight hour's endless dark sky, I see a soft glow flicker on from across the street.

I'm not alone.

Nonsense

You were there for me
undyingly

Was I there
enough for you?

Some speak
your name
And are quick
to blame
Lies they think
are true

I protest at once
please don't trust
Those lies
were never you

They turn their heads
safe in their beds
There's nothing
left to do

Your secret safe
none left to blame
Because now
there are so few

I know you tend
to a better end
In the ocean
oh how blue

I Forget You're There

The sharp pain reminds me
of your existence
As it radiates through my arm
you've made my vein your home

How long you'll stay
no doctor can say
If you were to grow
or move you know

That would be the end
of us both

No Option

The pain changed me

How could it not?

My home
went up in flames
My body
trapped inside

There is no
going back

That place
no longer exists
That person
no longer exists

Incineration

Sometimes all you can do
is watch yourself
Burn
and hope
That the best parts
of you
Survive and
become stronger

Dahlia

Like the flower
whose petals you
Pulled apart
you left me bare
Only a faint memory
of what I once was

Rebirth

Emerging from my
lifeless body
This new version
has risen
Ready to
create
Do
and
Be
Everything
my old self
Could not

No Longer Mine

How do I find the space within myself to hold this?
How do I create more of myself when the best
parts of me were obliterated?

I'm still grieving those parts of me that died
the parts of me that I want so desperately
To barge through my front door
saying that they're sorry for the delay
They just got lost along the way
home

It's the word *home* that rings in my ear
as I hit this one year
mark

What is *home*?
what does that word mean really because

I thought I knew

Home is where you should be safe and warm
not confused, lost, and torn
And I'm still pondering who I am
and why I can't stand
At this one year
mark

The nightmares of my screams
still haunt all my dreams
And I'm left wondering why
there's still no sun in my sky

I thought after all this time
I would be able to find
A glimmer of hope
through the fog and the smoke
A reason to smile, to say,
"just wait awhile, I'll be okay"
but no words like that can be heard today

All I feel is what I thought could never be real
a pain that cripples and lingers
And so my fingers reach for my medication
hoping for some sort of rectification
For what I lost

The pain still tosses me up and
drags me down
To a place of no sound
my screams now silent
As the water fills my lungs
slowly yet violent

I'm wasting away
as night turns to day
In a body that's no longer mine

It's the Things We Can Never Get Back That We Miss the Most

My body and mind have been working towards this day for so long. Now that it's here, it doesn't feel like a year. All aspects of my life have warped. I was able to pick up some of the pieces, but most were lost to the storm. Like a hurricane that passed over me, It has forced me into a desolate wasteland. All that's left are memories I believe to be true. Most things are misleading, like a mirage of water in the desert. Those parts of me look like how I used to be, but they do not function the same. I'm told they never will. I know I must make peace with the reflection of this new person, but I'm still searching within myself for the answer to "how?". No answers can be found in a brain trapped in a hazy den and my heart is still too heavy with sorrow to light the way.

This past year is nothing more than scattered chunks of time missing, blocked out by the medications and heartbreak of it all. When they ask me to reflect on this year, when they ask, "What was the pain like?" I no longer have hesitation to create comfort for those who have never watched their body die, who have never grieved something they can't replace.

The pain was like a fog. For so long I was left in darkness. Everything behind me was evaporating. Each day the song of joy for what was to come, fell silent. What was in front of me was unable to take shape. I stared into the abyss, waiting for any light to show itself. But there became no reason to have my eyes open, so the darkness took them as well.

The recovery has been a battlefield. Their bombs falling from the sky with fatal intentions. The flashes of light from impact are what lit their silhouettes. I watched as they faded into the smoke, walking across enemy lines. They returned home. They returned to their life, to their joy. They left me to bleed out in the trenches they created. The smoke burned my lungs and I fell back into the abyss. I lingered there, formless, nameless, alone, for an eternity.

It's the things I can never get back, that I miss the most. I've been searching for them, in the piles of debris, but my search parties have been in vain. The few rooms I've been able to clear out are being reinforced with new material. The concrete is still being poured into this new foundation. I don't know how long this will take, or what the end result will look like. It's still something I find myself avoiding. *The pain runs too deep.* The voice says.

As I sit among the ruins, I don't know which way to face. Do I look behind me and try to remember what I can? Or do I look ahead? How do I honor the death of myself without becoming lost in the grief and despair? Each evening, I ask the night sky my questions, but she has yet to reply.

Part II

The Invisible Wars

Chronic Illness

Enslaved to live
in a dying body
Our fate sealed

No bright future
before us no chance
We will be healed

Wondrous gardens from
our eyes are sown
Grief and loss are
our home

Doomed we are
to walk alone
Enslaved to our
dying bodies

They All Stood There

Each creature
stepping up
To take
their turn

Each one
their cold
Cruel eyes
lack concern

Each hand
a flame
They let
me burn

They all
stood there

The echo of
my screams
I could
no longer bear

Daydreams Fade to Reality

Majestic
looking out
Over the sea

Living in
a body
Of love
pain free

Able to do
all your heart
Desires
never knowing
The torture
of internal fires

Born into a
body determined

To burn
how to kill or
Love itself
it cannot discern

All hope is shattered
strength chased away
By the thought
of battling with
Yet another day

Spoken hope of a normal
tomorrow they cannot say
Within this body there
is no kind safe place to stay

Promises of a happy
ending they cannot make

From my body and
soul there is nothing
Left to take

What more can I do
for I wish not to run
If only I could
reverse the damage
That has been done

I Wonder Who You Would Have Been

I wonder who you would have been
and all the things you would have seen

Would you be short?
would you be tall?
Would you be big?
would you be small?

You'd live your life
just like a ball
You'd know your worth
and never fall

With all the starlight
in your eyes
Your presence would
light up the skies

The sun would smile
on your face
No sign of sadness
they could trace

Down upon you
like the glow
Of the moon
upon the snow

I wish I could
have seen you grow
But who you are
I'll never know

In the meadow
you would play
But all I see
is just a grave

For the soul
who's just a dream

I wonder who
you would have been

Infertility

Blue, brown, or green
I wonder what color
Would have reflected me

The heavens
would have shown in your beauty
The sun
in your kindness

All loving creatures would have
knelt at your feet
An Earth goddess
perhaps
A god of Neptune

Love in your heart
you would have kept

Grief in mine
I must accept

To have known you
would have been
To love you

To love you
would have been
To hold you

I am cursed
forsaken
Unable to do either

This lifetime will never
be ready for
You my darling

My body is a tomb
and nothing as pure
As loving as you
could grow in me

Black Moon

My connection
to the moon is not
a beautiful red river
celebration that arrives
every month

The moon only makes
her appearance with
the changing of the seasons
with a black pool of
seething agony

Reminding me that
my body is a desolate field
plundered by the same
thief who tried to rob
me of my womanhood

Lupron Injection

The sun shone brightly as if to mock me. The birds singing sweetly. There was a gentle breeze. The usually short walk from the parking garage to the building seemed longer today for some reason. Stepping into the elevator, "what floor?" asked an older gentleman with a brown cap and warm smile. "Three please, thank you" I said smiling back.

The walls of the waiting room are a soft pink color. The chairs worn. A young couple to my right very obviously excited for their bundle of joy to be. Another couple to my left already holding their own. "For Helen". I sprang up. Not out of excitement but out of wanting this ordeal to be over, to be back in my car and heading home. We entered the exam room, "okay, so when was the first day of your last period?" She asked as if that question wasn't a loaded gun. As if that question didn't slash its way through me. "Around the third week of June", I said. Her obviously confused facial expression due to the fact that it's now mid-October reminded me that this was not my usual nurse. "I have endometriosis", I said trying to sound as if it that word didn't break my spirit. "Oh. Okay, I see that in your chart here", she said in a cold, distant tone. "I'm sure you do" I thought to myself. "Well then, that explains your visit today. I'll go get what we need and come back". Before I could politely nod my head and say, "okay", she was out the door.

Within a few minutes she returned with the little death monster. "This might sting a little." Sting my skin? It definitely did that. But this needle also seared my soul with the reminder that I live in a disabled, loss filled body. That my temple is a tomb. It's the home of broken dreams and days filled with agony. I lay on my floor crying due to pain and the grief. I mourn who I would have been if it wasn't for this incurable creature. If it wasn't for this disease that tortures my body for pleasure.

Making my way back out through the waiting room is always filled with awkward glances from the glowing couples. I can see in their eyes that they wonder if I'm going to be facing the next nine months alone. Their looks of pity with a hint of distain always make me feel as though I need to defend myself, but I'm too exhausted to entertain them today.

I start the isolating walk back to the elevator. The journey back to my car is surprisingly longer than before. Perhaps it's the heaviness, the burden not only in my womb but in my heart and soul that make this walk never-ending.

Once I'm finally back in my car, I let out a sigh of relief. "Only two more shots", I say in my head, "This is almost over".

How naive I was to think that.

Starting my car, I feel the side effects of this round of chemotherapy. An immediate wave of dizziness with nausea overtakes me. The treatment has been crippling my body for the last four months.

Drained of everything I have, drowning in fatigue and sorrow, I leave the parking garage and start my journey home.

The Urge

The urge
overtakes my body
My mind numb
I can only focus
On my eyes

They scream at me
seeking both to
Be touched and
left alone

I try to fight my hand
but it's being forced to
My eyes as if
they're magnets and
My life depended
on them meeting
Reeking their havoc
having their way

It doesn't hurt
there's stillness
Here is where I
find the relief

or

The insatiable urge
still pulsing
Hungry for more
but with no prey left

A Fluid Moment

The green ivy, lilies, clouds, and warm winds bringing comfort from the cold are the moments of stillness and content. They're the moments when hummingbirds and butterflies pass me. It's when I can close my eyes and take a deep breath with clear lungs.

These moments are when I feel most at peace.
Neither the mania nor depression demanding
to be held.

If only this moment lasted forever.
If only this garden remained green and
full of life.

Mood Swing

What happened?
I was still me a moment ago

Why has the life
suddenly left my body?

A golden afternoon
turned into a pouring Sunday

This life doesn't suit me
no not anymore

It won't be this way forever
but you know it will

I don't have the energy
to fight this battle
But you cannot surrender

A Huntress with Her Prey

I cannot fight Her
not anymore

no
I say in My head
as I feel
cold
distant
angry

I go to scream
but nothing comes out
I try to run
but I
cannot escape Her

She takes over
My bones
My muscles
My mind

I'm drowning in Her

She drips with malice
She longs for pain

My mind resists
My thoughts remain My own
but not for long
they too will fog and warp and
change into what
She wants
My memories to become

She tears through My body
a huntress with Her prey
She rips open My soul
to slip into it
Herself

Whoever
She is
is not
Me

Mania Palace

Walls made of glass
sun surrounds her
Holds her

Ceiling flawed in contrast
burning desire engulfs her
Destroys her

Did she have a chance?

Shards of glass
in her body
Bleeding sunlight

A starlight fantasy
a summer dream
Burned too bright

Holes for her eyes
flames steal her sight

Lit up like a thousand stars
standing in her mania palace

The Place Between

The sun and moon are in constant flow with one another. Inescapable. Their dance never ceases. They move together. When one rises the other must fall to the background. The cycles of bipolar disorder follow the same rhythm of the sun and moon.

The sun is the mania, the natural high, and the unrealistic optimism. It's when there is no rain, no clouds, just the blinding golden light. It's the only thing you can focus on. It burns everything else to the ground as if it didn't exist. The heatwaves are the moments of unexplainable anger that flow freely without warning and without apology.

The moments of the shift are the eclipse. The moon begins to force her way to the forefront. Slowly and patiently consuming the sun and everything he created.

The moon and night are the depression, the darkness, the heaviness. Every dream, everything worked for, and everything once so deeply loved has disintegrated. It no longer exists, and it feels like it never did. Once again there is no point, no reason, no motivation. There's only the cold and manipulating sadness that masks itself as an old friend.

The back-and-forth battle within is when the day breaks and the night falls. The sun sets and the moon fades but their dance never stops. They never miss a step, never falter. The mania ends and the depression ends but their dance never will. They are in a constant battle to win. When one takes over, the other counts down until it regains control.

Both exhausting and overwhelming, yet neither care about the destruction they have each created.

Born of Two Worlds

Sometimes there are those who feel both, who see both, and who are both.

To feel such joy followed by immeasurable grief and sorrow haunted me. For a long time, I wanted to be anyone else. The highs were of blinding starlight, like fireworks lighting up the sky. Each thought exploding in my brain becoming the best possible idea I've ever had. I need more fuel, I'm creating masterpieces, I'm working until morning sleep is a thing of the past. I am the conductor, first chair violinist, a world-renowned harpist, and flute player. I am a critically acclaimed symphony all on my own. I'm giving my award winning and debut performance, people are in awe of me and standing in ovation, crying tears of happiness from the song I've just birthed into reality then right on cue

I am thrust from the rooftop of mania into the black void of depression. As I fall, I see each idea, each creative endeavor turn to stone. Each music note completely frozen into silence. Time will stand still in the world of mania, waiting for me to return. But in the black void, time is infinite. I will be tortured by my own mind for an eternity.

Passing Seasons

Pumpkin patches
dried leaves
Ghosts and ghouls

Memories in time of
childhood happiness
Now only mark a time
of pain sorrow and
Isolation

The smell of gingerbread
warm and comforting
A safe place to hide

The years passed by
safe places left to fade
All were ripped away
by the darkness
That remains

Fall

It was only in fall
once the leaves fell
With their last breath
it crept in slowly

With the winter cold I
could makes sense of
Why it lingered in death

Spring and summer were still safe
still untouched by darkness

How could this ever change?
when there's nothing but light
How could the darkness find its way in?

Betrayed by my own mind

What was once only fall and winter
was now every day
No matter if the flowers were in bloom
or frozen over
No matter if the trees were bare
or provided summer shade

The heaviness latched onto me
dragging me down

What was once only in the depths
of a cold cruel night
Was now with every breath
of warm summer air

When I watch flowers bloom
It does too
When I see the sunrise
It watches through my eyes

Lingering in Darkness

I have been frozen
for sometime
now

Stuck in ice
alone
cold and distant
quiet and reserved

I have been frozen
for too long
now

Shivering
watching my breath
leave my body

Wondering if the
warm sun
will ever again enter
my lungs

Or if I'm meant
to be this
frozen person
lingering in darkness

I Can't Keep Doing This

The same words
mulling around in my head
Echoing in my mind
learning to express myself
For the first time
no matter how hard I try
Nothing seems to come out right
I'm left on the bathroom floor
Trying not to cry
but *here we go again*
Says the little voice inside

End of the Day

My breath shallow
gently drifts away

My eyes dim
swallowed by night

My body slain
left to caress
The frozen ground

The Stranger in the Garden

The days were losing sunlight, the colors of the leaves were fading, and winter's frost was taking hold. I could feel it in me, the lingering sadness that arrives promptly at my doorstep each December like a subscription box. I decided to force myself outside before it became impossible. I put on my gray and blue sweater and began walking towards my secret scenic hideaway.

As I was reaching the outskirts of the garden, I noticed a woman with golden hair in a bright yellow dress sitting on the bench that I normally claim as mine for the day. As I was nearing the gate, she looked up at me with the warmest smile and kindest green eyes I had ever seen. She looked so familiar, but I couldn't place her. I didn't want to intrude on her time alone, but she invited me to sit next to her and we began talking. It was as if she was my best friend since childhood. She spoke to me about the Renaissance and the Fall of Babylon, Mount Vesuvius and Charlemagne. There was nothing she didn't know. After a few hours went by, I realized the time and needed to return home. She asked if she could see me tomorrow, "at the same time?", she said with a smile. "Of course, I wouldn't miss it", I said smiling back.

    She was waiting for me the next morning, this day seemed to mirror that of the previous. We talked for hours. It was as if time stood still. I was continuously mesmerized not just by what she said, but how she said it. The way she moved her hair behind her ear and how she wrinkled her nose when she laughed, made me feel like I had known her my whole life. The weeks went by, but my sadness seemed to be getting heavier. I was finding it harder to meet her each morning, but I didn't want to lose a new friend due to my own sadness. So, I continued to heave myself out of bed. Everything around me was fading, expect for her. Writing and painting were now mundane tasks. No longer did they bring me joy or excitement. Hearing her laugh was becoming my only chance of having a good day. Seeing her was the only thing I looked forward to in life. With her I had hope.

    I gazed out my window and saw the now bare branches swaying side to side. Everything in me was screaming, "stay in bed!" But I didn't want to give into my depression, so I started the exhausting process of getting up. The path to the garden seemed longer this morning. When I got to the gate, I noticed she wasn't there. I sat on our bench, thinking how odd it was for me to be early. I waited until the daylight ran out, but she never came. While trudging home, I began analyzing everything I did the day before. I wondered what I had done wrong, what I had said that pushed her away. I wasn't able to sleep that night. My body felt like it was laying on a thousand needles and I couldn't move.

The following day, I tried to get up, but it was impossible. My body was cement. My mind began blaming me for her not being there the day before. I couldn't escape the feeling of guilt that buried itself in my stomach. The more I thought about it, the more I couldn't breathe. I was frozen. "How could you be so stupid" the voice in my head kept screaming at me, "What did you say that made her never want to see you again?" I promised myself that no matter how I felt tomorrow I would walk to the garden and wait for her.

The next morning, I walked along the narrow winding path to the garden. The flower bushes now only thorns and the roses now all collapsed. But none of that mattered, I was able to breathe again. I saw her. Sitting in the same yellow dress on our bench. I quickened my pace towards her. She waved me over with her smile, but as I approached, she began to morph into a stranger I didn't recognize. No longer a beautiful woman with green eyes and golden hair, but a man with a sinister grin. I looked behind me and the path was gone. The garden was turning into a desert.

I found myself paralyzed with fear. Fighting the air to breathe, my body began shaking. This person who once gave me life was now revoking it. As he walked closer to me, each step he took turned a bone to lead. The ground started to engulf me. It was swallowing me whole. I tried to scream for help, but all that came out were gasps for air. "There's no one around to help you."he said with a smile that made my skin crawl.

Then there was only darkness and the echo of the man's laugh.

The next day, I called my psychiatrist. I told her how I started off okay and had hope, but out of nowhere the darkness came in faster than ever before. I told her how I physically couldn't get out of bed and that I couldn't breathe. That my dreams were now nightmares and all that I could see. She seemed surprised, "that's not usually how it goes with that", she said, "you were such a good candidate for it". There was a long pause, I knew she was trying to think of what to say next or what other options were available for me. Finally, she broke the silence with, "we could change the dose, maybe that would help?", but I wanted nothing more to do with it. I told her no. I laid in bed staring at my ceiling. I was defeated. My doctor had sold me on false hope. What seemed so perfect, became a living hell.

"Lithium is tried and true" kept ringing in my ear. But not for me. I met her in the garden of my mind, I tried to be her friend. But she betrayed me. She was not who she said she was. She desecrated my body with a smile on her face.

5150

Cold white walls
long drawn-out halls
Rooms fill with screams
they're just bad dreams

I say in my head
some here wish they were dead
Then they say how they've tried
it's all a blur in my mind

I say to myself
that this place isn't real
But I'm awakened by Agnes
throwing her meal

It's not a kind place
filled with laughter or joy

The drones flicker their eyes
always watching yet coy

Judging are their minds
their true words they dare not say
We all look out our windows
yearning to leave one day

These four white walls
with their drawn-out halls
Are not filled with hope
it's where we've been sent
Where they force us to rest
after we've tried the rope

Are You Done? Are You Fine?

What now? I ask in my mind
as they hand me my clothes
I have yet to find
the darkness in me
That was forced to be timed
seventy-two hours
Are you done? Are you fine?
they ask with stone faces
To see what I'll say
then Agnes starts screaming
"I...I'm okay"

A Bipolar Slumber

The moon and the sun
went for a run
To see who
could win

The sun hit a tree
the moon hit a star
And neither
felt they fit in

Their host did her best
but she finally confessed
That there was no light
she could see

She faded away
night turned to day
Gently she rests
now in peace

Remember Her
How She Used to Be

Remember her
how she used to be
A princess from a fairytale
a light that set love free

She often wished to talk about it
to make sense of what she's seen
But the silence had grown too loud
the sadness had grown too deep

It was something within her
like a twisted thorny vine
It overtook her brain and body
the voice told her, "say you're fine"

They say she did it on a whim
a spur-of-the-moment type thing
But they never really paid attention
now her favorite song they sing

No, they never seemed to notice
how her eyes began to fade
Her smile was now hollow
her body now decayed

I wish I would have known
is what they start to say
My house was always open
there she could have stayed

The warning signs they did not see
to her mind she was a slave
She followed its last decree
now they stand above her grave

So, remember her
how she used to be
She's in the morning light
she's the wind that moves the sea

The Storm is Coming

Endless blue sky
iridescent light
But my lungs
are wilting

My body is growing weak
my legs are useless
The sweet spring air
is turning sour

The warmth from
the sun fades
As I look to the horizon
I see it

The sky turns to ash
darkness eclipses the sun

The tide rises

engulfed in shadow
My shriveled lungs
are yet again plunged
Into this sea of agony

These storms
come without warning
They submerge me
to the depths of my pain

They torture my mind
creating a false world
A horror show
filled with only sorrow
And pain for sport

There is no escape from these storms
they know where I hide and
They know me too well

Part III

The Rise & Fall of Love

Brown Eyes

Dry eyes tell
more truths
Than the
sweetest of lips

My Body Sang for You

Like the sensual harp
that brings ecstasy
To every ear
that hears her song
My body was the
instrument of
Our love

Your hands
gently caressed
Each string
making the
Sweetest symphony
of sound

Even Apollo
came to see
Who was creating
such harmonies
For the gods

and what was the
Divine instrument
you were playing

Twin Flames

You were Ares
magnetic with an insatiable
Desire for pain mixed
with pleasure
A fire within you
that wanted to engulf
Every inch of me
slowly burning your
Way up my body

I Athena
expert at destroying
All things dear to me
launching my attack
With a single word
summoning my legions
To the battlefield
with one look

We together were Chaos
our bodies intertwined
Through lifetimes and
each time we find
Cosmic ecstasy

Questions

Resting my head on your chest

What are you doing?
you asked

I was
listening
Feeling

The heartbeat
that mine
Lived for

I was
holding on
To the rhythm

So that one day
when this is just a memory
I'll close my eyes and return here

What are you doing?
you asked

Nothing
I said

Games

I thought it would be grand
the universe at bay
I thought it would be joyous
the devilish games they play

The tragic game had ended
his body left to stay
His soul now ascended
the devilish games they play

When it was said and done
stone cold was her face
Two beating hearts now one
the devilish games they play

So now is she lonely
so now does she say
Beware of the young lovers
and the devilish games they play

There's No Escaping Them

Every evening, as the light goes out, it happens. She feels them at the same time. The wholehearted and exhaustive love she has for him and the devastation of his loss.

With a Heavy Heart

He said as I sat there
yes my heart was heavy
Yet it was so much more

It was pierced by too
many knives
To count

It was cold
as if winter had come early
Freezing my body

It was broken
as if it would
Never beat again

It was lost
wondering
How long it would
have to wait
to see You

My body ached
not only for
You
but for
My Heart
to understand

To know that You
were gone

My mind told
my heart
To forget

But my heart told
my mind and soul
That it could never
forget

With a heavy heart
we are gathered here today

He said as I sat there

Where You Remain

My eyes
will never be able to see
You again

My ears
will never be able to hear
Your laugh again

My arms
will never be able to feel
Your caress again

but my heart

My heart will see
You in the city lights

My heart will hear
Your voice in the songs we sang

My heart will feel
Your presence in the silent moments
where now there's only echoes of loneliness

My heart will tell
You how much You meant to me

Although to my eyes, ears, and arms
You are gone
in my heart
You will remain

Dreams

When I close my eyes
I see you
just the same
warm smile that outshone the sun
You haven't changed

When I close my eyes
I hear you
just the same
whimsical laugh that lit up my world
You haven't changed

When I close my eyes
I feel you
just the same
loving embrace
You haven't changed

Too Soon

May your heart
not know the pain of
Love's separation

Too soon
for
Too soon

Is the hour
that turns lovers
Into enemies
and song into
Tears

Moving On

Memory
distant and cold
Memory
a false love sold

Premonition
bright and bold
Two hearts yielding
to love untold

In clear waters
hearts set ablaze
Eyes of mist
and clouded days

In another life
an ash filled haze
A dark twist
a new lover's gaze

Strange Places

How strange to find a happy place
when all I know is sadness

I feel with my heart
the depths and
Darkness of the ocean

Yet here you are
the Light
Warm and kind

You are foreign but
not unwanted

You are different
yet feel like
Home

Honest Affection

Green eyes
gazing around
gazing down

He runs his hands through his hair
he bites his lip

We only keep eye contact
for a brief moment

His arms
could hold me up or
pin me down with ease

His hands
throb they yearn to caress my thighs
until his fingers find a much sweeter place
to touch me tenderly

He enters me
with his eyes

He says all the right things
his body says more than his mind
but I'm left wanting more

Wanting to know if
his love
his affection

Is real
is honest

Or does he too
want to kiss my body
run his hands through my soul
and after he screams my name

Leave
onto his next conquest

Blinded by Desire

To have been left in the dark for so long
Makes this light feel unreal

I wonder how long the glow will last
I wonder if you'll stay

Will you be like the others?

Clinging to the idea of me
Not wanting the reality of me

Your Reflection

It was not me
that you loved
You loved
yourself in
Pieces of me

You saw your
own reflection
In my body
and thought
That was love

The day came
where all you
Could see
in me
Was a reflection
you hated

And so
your love for me
Turned into
loathing of yourself
Our love together
once vivacious
Now lifeless

Lies of A Moonlight Walk

Disingenuous love stained the lips
that once made love to yours
Making plans for
a moonlight walk

Lies from your lips
now stain mine
Shallow hearts know
no shame
Dark twisted games
they play

But I too
hold my own secrets
Deep within my soul

The aching to find the one
who can hold them
Overtakes my body like

the light of the moon
When she is her most full and tempting
when she caresses the earth with
Her loving gaze

I walk beneath her light
wondering if she can see
All the lies you spoke to me

Restless

You found me when I was restless
looking for something
not sure of what

I found you when you were lonely
looking for someone new
something different

The connection was undeniable
for a moment I was your favorite person
for a moment I was your everything
for a moment it was real
only for a moment

Soon the sweet nothings
became stale and crumbled

There was nothing left
only empty space

You came in so fast
demanding my attention
creating your place in my world

Then you left
and your place shattered
into a thousand pieces

There I was
deciding to keep this
space you created
and make it my own

or

Go back to the way I was
without you
without this extra room full of
broken promises and regret

I paid the price for giving you my attention

When I hear your name
I only think of
Regret
Mistake
Disappointment

Not yours but my own
my own regret of not listening to myself
my own mistake of saying yes
my own disappointment in hoping that you
would be different

Forest

you were the most vivid green
i walked for miles in your meadows
your countless acres of woods
were my home for so long

but i got lost in your forest
and i couldn't find my way back
i became so intertwined with your world
that i forgot my own

i saw you walking towards me
i thought you were coming to
cut me out of your vines so
i could breathe again
be me again

but you walked right through me

to catch her

i lost myself in you
while you were busy
losing yourself in someone else

Piece of You

They threw away a piece of you, so you threw that piece away too.

Fragments

How foolish am I
to have believed your words
Of comfort saying you were
ready for new love
When the memories of her laugh
and her beauty were still
Alive in your mind

When you said
I love you
I should have known it
was not to me that you
Spoke those words
it was to the parts of me
That reminded you of her

That Part of Me

Words waiting to be spoken
the tension rising like the
The Red Sea tide

My heart faded to be broken
your words cut through me
Creating rivers for eyes

What I'd give to return this deceitful
potion overflowing with your lies
A warm summer day faded
to gray and black skies

Your energy had me
mesmerized but how I wish
I would have listened to
the little voice inside

Before the first words
were ever spoken
I could have saved
the part of me that died

Hollow Bones

In my hollow bones
there once were daises
growing from my body
towards the light of your soul

In my hollow bones
there once was music
that played for me and you

In my hollow bones
there became a coldness
that froze the daises

In my hollow bones
there became a silence
that drowned out the music

It was a Sunday
when I felt the life
return to my hollow bones

I heard a new melody
growing towards my own light

My First Home

He was
my home but
It was no
place of comfort

No he never
smelled of fresh baked cookies
No he never
kept the space warm with laughter

The paint was chipped
a deadly chill
Danced through the air

It was filled with
water damage
A busted radiator
fuming with jealousy and deceit

It was in a nice neighborhood but
you could see the cracks
In the foundation
from the street

To All Who Say Love is Dead

His eyes are the deepest galaxies
His face is so lovely
Aphrodite melts in his presence

For he is built like the gods themselves
who is he to the mortal world?

He is
Passion
Desire
Wanting

To be near him is to love him
to bear witness to him is ecstasy

Loss

It was a feeling
that came on so suddenly
an indescribable sadness

A part of me
that had left all at once

I couldn't breathe

I was paralyzed

I couldn't think straight

I felt lost

Then it hit me
this was loss

I felt it in every bone
of my body

You
were gone

That Morning

That morning was still. Not how I was expecting it to be. There were no birds singing. There was no movement of the trees. The wind was holding her breath to ensure those last few moments were not disturbed. That morning was cold. The looming clouds kept the sun at bay as the rain set in.

That morning two hearts became one.

That morning I realized that the world slowed down, the birds were quiet, the wind stood still to keep everything the same for one more day. As if they knew what was about to happen. For one more moment I could see what you saw, feel what you felt. Before that morning there was you. Your warmth. Your kindness. Your love. After that morning there was coldness, sorrow, agony.

I find myself closing my eyes often. I take myself back to that morning. I woke up next to you. I can still feel your right arm pulling me closer. How my heart has cried to feel the same as it did with you.

That morning.

You

For the longest time, the reminder of you was everywhere demanding my attention. The reminder of you felt like a thousand knives stabbing my soul. The reminder of you felt like my heart shattered into a million pieces spilling across my floor. One night became a year. The soft glow of moonlight became a midnight darkness. As if the moon knew to no longer shine a familiar light because your light was gone. For the longest time I was angry and confused. I felt emptiness where I once felt you. I tuned myself out. I turned myself off.

A shift came one morning. I woke hearing the sounds you loved so much. Instead of rushing to turn them off, instead of turning me off, I paused in the familiar sound as if you told me, "Wait! You once loved this too. We once loved this together."

You are gone. As much as it hurts, I cannot change it. But now I pause, I listen, I remember. The sting of your absence remains, but the wounds are healing slowly. I hear you in the doves singing outside my window. I feel you in the gentle breeze. I see you waiting for me in my dreams. The only place where I know you will be.

Longing

My heart and soul still ache for you

They wait to feel
your touch
your warmth

They wait to see
you smile

But they must make do
with the memory of your laugh and
lingering caress of your touch

Another World

She will speak
your language

Your parents will love
and adore her

You will wonder how you managed to
live without her

She came to you in a dream
she came to you from another world

I Could No Longer Breathe for the Both of Us

It started as a single candle flame.

A soft flicker, a warm golden glow of curiosity and excitement. Over time, our glow became brighter, nearly iridescent. It showed the world that we loved each other with a burning passion. But as the seasons changed, our glow was becoming too bright, too hot. It was growing, changing into something I did not recognize. It was no longer a light of life, warmth, and love. It was of destruction. The flames of hell. With tears running down my face, I saw what was once a candle of hope become an inescapable wildfire that blocked the sun and killed everything in its path. Ash filled my lungs turning them black with tar, and I could no longer breathe for the both of us.

September

Melting the frost of your love from my body took years. I served out my sentence. I am no longer your sun. I am free to love myself with the passion you never could. With the sensuality and desire you denied me, I warm my own body. I feed my own love.

I Wanted to Tell You

You came to me in a dream last night
there was life in your body
there was light in your eyes

You held my waist and
kissed my neck gently

You took me back
to the moment when you told me
that death was now within you
and your days now so few

Your smile faded
your eyes dimmed
your body dissolved in my arms

How real that moment was
with you

When I awoke
I wanted to see you and
tell you about my dream

But how foolish am I
to have forgotten
that it's only in
my dreams that
we meet

Us

Let's say what we actually were my love, two children pretending to be adults. I was closed off to my feelings, trying so desperately to push them back down. Yet every time I saw you the most orgasmic rush of joy would come over me. The ecstasy surging through my veins pulled me closer to you. But my past traumas kept you at bay. You could never truly get through to me. I never let my walls down long enough for you to launch a successful campaign.

You, were ignoring your feelings. Wanting so desperately for them not to be real. You hoped that meeting me could be stricken from your memory. You heart had never felt like that, but your past traumas had convinced you that love wasn't real. So, you too kept walls up that I couldn't break down, not even with my best warriors.

We could have been real. We were so close to being real. We were so in love, but with such stubborn hearts. Everything you did was wrong. Everything I did wasn't enough.

We both wondered why we weren't fitting together like in all of the movies we went to see. They all fit so well, like missing puzzle pieces, but not you and me. We couldn't make each other fit. We screamed each other's names at the same time and then stood there in silence looking at each other blankly. We each waited for the other to talk first. But silence was the only thing we could hear.

We shattered our dreams and expectations of each other and our relationship. We created a reality of nightmares fluent in misunderstanding. But we never really spoke about it, how we should have.

We never talked about it to resolve it. We just pretended not to see the mess we were creating.

In those last moments, we both found that love is not always enough.

Dealbreakers

Your eyes tsunamis
my own the dead sea
Our hearts both
breaking

Your look cut
through my soul
My own gaze
piercing yours

Together both
drowning inside
The home we spent
years building

This dream come true
sinking to the depths
Of the ocean
by both our hands

Imprint

During daylight
two ex-lovers

But when the moon
starts her tease show
For the stars

Your body aches
for my sweetness
For my warmth to
open for you
The way the flower
opens for the bee

Your hands take their time
tracing down my spine

I can't deny
how my body trembles
Underneath yours

You can't deny
that no matter how
Hard you try
your body could
Never forget mine

The Sweetness of Spring

Keeping the gaze of
your brown eyes
In mine
you cannot deny
That you
are a hummingbird
Drinking the sweetest nectar
you will ever find

If You See My Work, Read This One

In those days filled
with warm summer air
In those nights filled
with endless starlight
I believed I loved
you fully

Not until years later
did I discover
The true depths
of my love

You deserved this love
we deserved this love
I was not ready
and for that
I am sorry

Somehow You Know

It's been so long
but the thought of what
Went wrong
still haunts me

I think about what
we could have been
If I was who I am
today back then

I wonder if you've changed
just as much as me
But my mind mustn't wander
so I leave you in a daydream

It's not safe to linger
in made up memories
Picnics in the garden
between the willow trees

It's strange but when I feel the wind
she takes me back in time
The lights along a winding road
of memory and rhyme

Now that's where I find myself
living to fall asleep
A made-up land is where I go
it's the only place we meet

In a circus by the sea
no sight of clouds nearby
It's only you and me
and a made-up lullaby

I see our younger selves
full of hope and mystery
Back when we were both open
wearing our hearts on our sleeves

Then I'm taken to our castle
among the rolling green hills
We're older now our bodies worn
we've experienced life's thrills

We never want for more
but that's when I wake up
My body pressed against the door
grasping a broken cup

All that's left is a heart
that was ripped apart
Now it's strung out on the floor
in bits and pieces
So I try with new adhesives
to make it beat like before
But it won't go back together
because it broke off at the core

Tell me you moved on and I
will lie and say the same
I'll erase you from my memory

and with it all the pain

Tell me so I can let you go
grasping what's not there
Holding onto smoke that's
evaporating in the air

Is killing me
slowly

I need to let you go
to make peace with this
In my dreams and somehow
hope you know

The days pass by in a hazy blur
a warmth is melting all the snow
How I feel has never changed
and yet I feel somehow you know

English 100

The winding pathway was once lined by nature's love notes not ready to meet the summer air. The benches were not built yet, so we sat by the creek, the river's moving tears. When spring came running home, the roses began to bloom. Red, yellow, pink, and purple the garden's fertile womb. Yet one morning a frost came without warning, and our garden was frozen in time.
It sat empty for years, yet you could still hear the roses that quietly cry. Too much time has passed on, they've started to decay. With them all the memories of us began to wash away. The garden was our secret meeting place, where we spent every day. The colors once so vibrant, faded all to gray.

It's been so long, but something has drawn my heart near. A higher power has summoned me back to this garden we once shared. As I walk along the dirt path, the garden has grown as well. I feel her heavy heart, she asks me not to dwell. The flower's tears have watered their own soil. The vines among the trees, the dark willow greens, wrapped tightly in a thorny coil. The most vibrant colors I thought I'd never see again, take me back to when you were mine. I close my eyes, to see you, to see us back in time. The iron statue of the long lost lovers is what we used to be. When we had no troubles, when it was only you and me. I'm fixing up our bench, I sit on it alone. The scent of irises and lilies have guided me back home.

Divine Timing

I've known you all this time
deep within my own mind
You have been waiting

I did not know what love is
until I gazed upon your soul
Until I had your hand to hold

When I close my eyes I find
our souls together intertwined
A new world we are creating

Part IV

The Place Where Great Spirits Meet

Where Great Spirits Meet

A spring meadow
of tall sweet grass
Sunrays everlasting
the sparrow's melody
Of joy and harmony

This is where great
spirits meet
Where human souls
do try to seek
The universe
broad and deep

This is where great
spirits play
Where human souls
do wish to stay
Among the sparrows
and sun rays
But it's not our
place to keep

Garden

How beautiful
the trees
Light coming through
the branches

How beautiful
the bees
Whispering love poems to
the flowers

Chamomile and Daffodils
in bloom
Lilies and Daturas
reaching towards the moon

Life standing still for the walker
life continuously moving for the watcher

Daises

There was nothing in this world
I would not have done for you

Like the daisies in your garden
I was a white and golden sun kissed hue

You were my North Star but
I let you rip my soul in two

And now just like your daises
our love filled days left right on cue

Stung

Do you think
the flower stays stung
By the bee who leaves
and does not return the
Next spring day?

Do you think the flower weeps
and cries out its name?

If the flower wilted or dared
not to bloom
The sun would weep
for the flower
Died too soon

The flower
among all things is
Pure and everlasting
she stands still

Under the sun
basking

Reminded of her beauty
the meadow sings
Her song

A new bee
will kiss her tenderly
She need not wait long

Spring's Return

Life is coming back
to the flowers

Yesterday I heard
a few of spring's bees
Knocking at my window
longing to come in

Oh what it would be like
to be a creature of spring
Surrounded by beauty
immersed in the sunshine

The vivid colors of life surrounding you
never knowing the darkness and
Depths of a winter night
where there's nothing but
The cold and inescapable loneliness

Mother Wind

Mother Wind of change
is howling to shed
All of your layers
release to her
The parts of you
holding your purpose back
Let her sweet air enter
your soul with the same
Force as Mother Sea
allow her to release
All your earthly bonds
allow your soul to be free

Three Rivers

I sat and stared
out into the night
There was nothing
to compare
You were out of sight
with no more care
All I felt was fright
with no other choice I
Turned towards the light

Autumn Light

That last sunset with you
was a kaleidoscope of autumn light

Orange and red danced
in a way I'll never forget

Engulfed in endless color
you were a beautiful sight

Every year when I return to where we met I
see the same sky that cried out our names

Even after all this time I hope you know I
still have all our pictures in their frames

In a Field of Lilies

A field of lilies in bloom
Your smile radiating up to the moon
Your laugh etched on my heart
I'll keep you there and
We'll never part

Forget-Me-Not

To know you've moved on and
now I've done the same
Somehow brings me happiness
instead of bringing pain

There are days where I still hear you
calling out my name
But now it's just a whisper
something I can tame

The day will come completely
when you no longer stain
My heart blue and purple
my love no longer strained

Yet often do I wonder
if I ever call your name

In an evening slumber
or during pouring rain

Roots

You're allowed to change and grow
to find new meadows to call home

With the seasons you too
will change and be reborn

Walk along the great rivers
dance under the moon
Feel the sun warm your spirit
it's time to break free of your cocoon

Part V
The Sacred Goddess

Fire Woman

Fire Woman
her body moves with ease
lighting up the darkness
next to loving seas

Fire Woman
dancing through the night
releasing all ego
releasing clouded sight

Fire Woman
her love is everlasting
her strength is letting go

Fire Woman
is every woman
moving to and fro

Air Woman

Air Woman
her love moves
through the trees
her embrace
carries all wings

Air Woman
waves hello
as she gently
settles snow

Air Woman
blows away all
your fears
and ego

Air Woman
is a force
both gentle
and strong

Air Woman
reminds you that
here is where
you belong

Earth Woman

Earth Woman
rooted in divine
creation

Earth Woman
grows love to
new elevations

Earth Woman
makes love to
the sun

Earth Woman
knows we are
all one

Water Woman

Water Woman
flows in deep harmony
with the universe
and all that is

Water Woman
from her body
flows divine bliss

Water Woman
is deep within
consciousness

Water Woman
creates all that lives

Trust

What good would you giving up do? You're standing on the brink of a breakthrough. You need to turn the page. You can't give up now or stay locked in your cage. All your ideas and passions will run away like the tears that soak your eyes, the ones that always stay.

You feel it in your body, in your soul. There is no going back, not anymore. You're divinely supported, heaven is opening the door. You need only to step through it, to touch your divine purpose, to feel it at your core. This is something you can do, trust me dear one, it's just like putting on a shoe. At first a little difficult, but now it's done on cue.

Trust in the divine angels, trust in your guides. Trust in the rain, trust in clear blue skies. Dear one, it's time to dry your worried eyes. It's time to take inspired action and release all the lies you've sold yourself so far on why it's, "just not the right time". You don't need to have it all figured out or to know how. But you must believe that what you seek is unfolding for you now.

Specifics

did you not ask for a miracle?
did you not ask to be absolved of all fear?

to be cleansed
to be purified

you asked for all things to be made right
you asked for your needs to be met

but it was
you
that never went into
how
you wanted things done

the universe
will respond to you
but it is up to you
to tell her how

Or

your fate will be
in the hands of a trickster
and she will have
her fun

Growth

This is not the ending of your life. This is the beginning of the next phase. This is growth. Overwhelming, exhausting, undeserving, but necessary. Let it push you to the next level. Let it fuel your desire to become successful. To become who you were destined to be. We die every time we advance to the next chapter in our book. Don't let that scare you. Take control of these new pages. Rise out of your own ashes. Do what you are called to do. Be who you were born to be. This is not the end dear one, this is the beginning.

Scorpio Full Moon

This is it
this moment
right now

Rise
Be
Create
Let go

You cannot be who
you were born to be
if you keep living
like who you
were yesterday

Release her
that's not you anymore

Freedom

On the day when you
can truly release them
When you can genuinely
let it go and no longer
Hoard your forgiveness
you will find on that day
You are finally free

Rise

When It takes
everything
from you
Rise
out of your
own ashes
Embrace
whole heartedly
this new
version of yourself
that you had
No choice in becoming

Warrior

    She's a warrior. A tired warrior, but one nonetheless. She knows her strengths but most importantly, she knows her weaknesses and where she can improve upon herself. She fights for a better world every day. She used the rocks they threw at her to build her castle. Each battle scar she has is a reminder of her worth and her place in this world. From her battle shield grows strength. From her sword grows courage. She leaves a legacy of valor, justice, truth, and love. She will always be fighting alongside you.

She Is All Things

She is the light and dark in everything
she is both sound and silence
she is a sunrise and moonlight

Her strength is reflected in her beauty
her beauty is reflected in her kindness
her kindness is reflected in her actions

She walks among stars in faraway galaxies
she exists in all realms as all things

Love

She first believed herself
to be too giving
To be too willing
to share her soul

She allowed herself
to be shattered
In hopes of her pieces
making others whole

As the seasons passed by
the false promises and
Low quality lovers
took their toll

One night the moon
told her that it was not

She who plunged love
into a dark lonely sea

It was the boys
who were not ready to be
Men and support her as
she sets her soul free

Create

The modern-day tragedy is that of people believing they don't have the power to create the life they want. They hand their soul over without a second thought. Too scared of success or failure, they never follow their heart. They sit at a desk, tucked in a corner for forty years helping someone else achieve their dream for the price of forgetting their own.

Don't let that become you. You deserve so much more than that life. Everything you need to create your dream life and reality are already within you. Don't be afraid of yourself. Don't be afraid of your own power.

You are the creator of your world. Make a world of what you love. With the sea below and warm sky above. Make a world where you know you are always enough. With a wish filled night and heaven's white dove.

Honesty

Great teachers teach from their experience. Great lovers love as if never broken. Great gardens are sown with the tears of the sky. Your greatness stems from your experiences, both good and bad. Do not let your past traumas or future anxieties hold you back from living your life fully and authentically.

Cycles

Your life isn't falling apart
it's falling into place

You're scared because you've never been here
this is a new version of you
This is unfamiliar territory

At some point you will cycle out of here too
but make sure you've learned all there is before
The next cycle shift occurs

Make the most of summer
before you settle into fall

Reminder

It is your responsibility
to cut them out
To let them go
to remove yourself from
Toxic situations and relationships
no one can do it for you

This is your sign
they're not worth it
The time you spend wishing
they were different or that they
Would respond is time taken
away from you
From your hopes and dreams

Don't pause your life
for someone who doesn't
Want to be in it
you will never move forward

Regret

Don't wait until it is with
your dying breath
That you tell them
how you feel

We all know
time isn't promised
And love is the
only thing that's real

You Are Enough

Honor who you are and
all you've accomplished
Live in the knowledge that
you deserve to be here
Exactly as you are

Purpose

I don't think finding our purpose in life is always meant to be easy. Yes, for some people it is. As soon as they took their first step, and inhaled their first breath, they knew what they were placed on this earth to do. For others, like myself, it is a continuous journey of self-exploration. Of opening one door, walking down ten hallways, only to open a hundred more doors. It doesn't matter how old you are, follow what your heart is telling you. Tap into your intuition and see where it guides you. You might have many purposes in this life, you might have one, embrace it. All of it. Because like the hummingbird who plays a vital role in the sweet symphony of life, you too are of great importance. It is up to you to explore and find your own flowers of purpose. So that you live in your own lush, vivid garden of life, overflowing with joy and radiance.

You Deserve to Be Happy

I hope at the end of the day, you're happy, proud, and at ease with who you are and what you do. If you are not, I hope that come the following morning you find the fire of resilience, strength, and determination that has always been within you to begin anew.

How Do You Celebrate Yourself?

Tell me about the moments
that broke you
Talk to me about the moments
where you fell apart

Show me the darkest places
in your mind
The places you keep hidden
from everyone else

What keeps you up at 3am?
what memories still haunt you?

Tell me about your doubts and your fears

then tell me how you overcame them

How do you recognize your achievements?
how do you celebrate yourself?

Start Acting Like It

It's okay to be scared, but don't let being scared make you turn away. Don't let being scared turn you into someone you don't want to know, someone you're not proud of. What does fear need to teach you? Like a mother wolf protecting her young, assume the role of the fierce nurturer and protector of yourself.

Show up on the days when it's the hardest. When all you can think about is the past and how the pain still haunts you. It's on those days that you need to show up for yourself more than ever. People don't have mental breakdowns on phenomenal days when all the planets are aligned and the angels are visibly supporting them.

It's on those days that we see the work that needs to be done. Maybe it's old work you thought was finished, maybe it's a new wound.

But don't you ever believe for a second that you're alone in this. Your guides have never abandoned you. Your soul is still within you. As much as you don't want those memories, they're a part of you. As much as you wish it didn't happen, it did. As much as you wanted them to stay, they left.

Your job is to still move forward. Your job is to sit with the pain. Your job is to love yourself so fucking much that your angels get jealous because not even they can love you that much.

Your job is to carry ALL parts of yourself forward. To protect your energy. To enjoy the bad days with the good, why? Because you're still breathing, you still feel the warmth of the sun, you still see the stars every night before you go to sleep.

So, cry, scream, sob - get it out, but still move forward. You always have the choice to lay down and be a victim, or show up for yourself like the Goddess you are. It's no one else's responsibility to make you think you're enough. You have to know you are and start acting like it.

I Hope You Choose You

Each of us are faced
with a pivotal moment
Where we must decide
to go forward in life or
Stay stagnant and let
our dreams fade away

This decision might
demand a response
During daylight
or 3am
It might happen at 20
or 42

Whenever this decision
must be made in your life
My god I hope
you choose to go forward

No matter how daunting
no matter how difficult it is

I hope you choose
you

Dear Little Me,

I see your red eyes and shirt soaked with tears. I still hear the words they called you. I still remember how it feels and how we started skipping meals. But if we don't let this go, we're never going to grow. Our life will pass us by, we'll be forever stuck up in the sky. We'll get lost in memory and never know who we could be.

It's been far too long but the time has come. I know you're afraid but the bells have rung. They're asking us to trust in something we can't see. I thank you for keeping us safe, but now it's time to be free. You've been through so much, too much and you want to stay hidden away. But I know you feel it within you, we can't hide from it, not another day. We can't stay in this box forever, as comfortable as it may be, it will hurt us in the end like a cup of scalding tea.

There's something new we must tend to. With every fiber of my soul I know this is a new path we must walk. One where we are whole. The wounds they inflicted upon us are scars now, they will always be with us. But please don't be afraid, we're made out of stardust.

Although I wish I could erase them from our skin, unfortunately I cannot. But through all of the healing phases, strength is what they taught. If you really think about it, without them we'd be strange. We wouldn't be who we are at all, in fact we'd have to change. Each scar is a reminder of what we went through to stand this tall. We dance to our own music at our own ball.

Things will arise that may open up our old scars, but that won't be the end of us, for we sit amongst the stars. The only way is up my dear, please don't be scared. I'll fix the ribbons in your hair and I'll always be right here.

The Longest Journey Home

Looking at my old photos was like looking at a stranger. The needs and wants of that person were so trivial. I didn't recognize her. Her hopes and dreams are distant and faded. Nothing more than an echo of a whisper. It's not something I missed nor something that made me sad, but realizing that I didn't know myself at all, became the longest journey home.

About the Author

Helen began writing poetry and won her first poetry contest when she was ten, nearly two decades ago. In her late teens, she began experiencing extreme depressive and manic episodes. Unbeknownst to her at the time they were due to bipolar disorder type one. Not sure what to make of these catastrophic mood swings, Helen did what she loves best - explore her emotions through writing.

Her work as a whole tends to stay on the darker, heavier side of life. The reader sees this in, *Remember Her How She Used to Be* and *5150*. Other poems like, *A Huntress with Her Prey*, gives the reader a glimpse into a rage filled and detached manic episode. Mixed episodes also made their way onto the page in, *The Place Between*.

Like many poetry collections, themes of love and grief are felt deeply within this body of work. *With A Heavy Heart, That Morning*, and *I Wanted to Tell You*, reflect the pain of losing a soulmate.

The creative forces behind the majority of the collection stem from Helen's mental health battles with bipolar disorder one and her multiple chronic illnesses: endometriosis, trichotillomania, and interstitial cystitis. Helen's two rounds of chemotherapy and two laparoscopic surgeries sparked, *I Wonder Who You Would Have Been*, *Infertility*, and *Lupron Injection*. The poem, *They All Stood There*, shares what it's like to live in a body that is plagued with multiple creatures (illnesses) determined to torture and kill you.

Despite these conditions, the catalyst for The Collective *A Soulful Mind* was a traumatic physical injury she sustained in March 2020. The opening poem, *Post Surgery*, brings the reader into her new, unwanted, reality filled with a symphony of knives, sleepless nights, and dark creatures about to feast on her body.

Outside of writing, Helen is a proper tree-hugger and animal rights advocate. She is also a Reiki Master, sound healer, and certified 500hr therapeutic yoga teacher. She's finishing her B.A. in Human Development and will be pursuing an M.A. in Existential Psychotherapy. She has a private healing & counseling business where she helps women redefine, "chronically ill" through holistic modalities.

Connect with Helen

Instagram: @authorhelenrigby

Facebook: @authorhelenrigby

Website: www.helenrigby.org

Made in the USA
Coppell, TX
21 August 2021